the arc of our dance with desire

OPEN HEART SUTRA SURGERY

stephen roxborough

NeoPoiesisPress.com

ℛ

NeoPoiesis Press, LLC

2775 Harbor Ave SW   Inquiries:
Suite D   P.O. Box 38037
Seattle, WA 98126-2138   Houston, TX 77238-8037

NeoPoiesisPress.com

Stephen Roxborough – Open Heart Sutra Surgery
ISBN 978-0-9892018-0-3 (pbk)
    978-0-9892018-3-4 (hardcover)
    1. Poetry. I. Roxborough, Stephen. II. Open Heart Sutra Surgery.

Library of Congress Control Number: 2013949976

First Edition

Cover, design and typography: Milo Duffin and Stephen Roxborough
Author photo courtesy of Jeff Pew

Printed in the United States of America

to the goddesses of attraction distraction
& endless chain reaction
to the glowing nymphs of kiss & whisper
to symbols of passion & the vibration of saints
to the hungry ghosts who haunt our deepest secrets
to our holy holy lady of perpetual lust

to the punitive gods of aversion & repulsion
to the essential eros of taste & touch
to the heart-stopping wonder
of line & form
& eye of the beholder

to our sweat & purr & lick & lap
our groans & moans & knowing & unknowing
& all our perpetual animal instinct
from each subatomic pulse to the cosmic big bang
to you & me & she & he & every One of us
moving into & through this mad galactic
dervish swirl of eternal dance

i love you i love you i love you

desire takes many forms
including
f o r m l e s s n e s s

a demon a goddess a want a toy a title a prize
a bauble a smile a bite a compliment
a relationship a fantasy a number
a regression an obsession a love a lust
a lost a key a date a drink a smoke
a dream a kiss a hug a portal
an angel
& sometimes a fall
from grace

desire tempts us taunts us feeds us
    bleeds us inspires us tests us wakes us
        shakes us molds & shapes us
            & time after time shows us
   who we are

open heart sutra surgery is the arc
of my dance with desire

   your dance awaits

stephen roxborough
anacortes 2013

Contents

good morning desire

i want to float across your
inner mongolia
& whisper fluent camel
on the steppes of your ears i want
to tattoo myself with your compassion
& embrace a million inkless
memories i want
to trespass on your forbidden
territories & drink from all
your deep secret
forest dreams

o want o passion
o lust
o dust o longing o crave
my hunger my ache i want
to trace your lips
with mine

then paint your open thighs
with sigh
& tranquil song

perfect plummeting

o to fall in love with you
fall spring summer winter in love
with you
free fall in love
with you
into you inside you through you inside me
falling falling deeper
with every breath
of your nonstop sky
deeper into the myth & truth of you
into the mindless
abyss of us

full of hungry happy sacred
laughing kisses
i want to fall
in dreams
with you

never wake up
fall down down down
so far down
we come out the other side
where everything us
is innocent
faultless
blameless complete

fused universal eternal
perpetual perfect
fallen grace

excellent surrender

      conquer my mind with kind
bursts of words

capture my flag with the rhythm of your breath
undress my subconscious
build a bonfire
with all my uniforms
& masks

      raise a bridge to heaven
with the heave of your hips

      from tender nape
to dangerous dimples
in the small of your immaculate
back i want you
dear desire
to conquer every possible
inch of me

      in every state
of landscape & mind

the pursuit of liberty

let me set your inner animal free
unlock the doors of pleasure
& pain

open your darkened windows
dissolve the bars of body

unspring
every mindtrap

break the time tempered chains
of self-doubt

release your ageless
wild spirit
into limitless sky

uncontainable

i want the everything of us

the planet of us
the one universe of us

how content our minds our prayers
our eyes hands lips
our accordion ardor expanding
& contracting
to suit
our tune & mood

how we part without parting
or falling apart

how we swell to fill the other up
how we fall into each other
how we relax
simply
into the easy chair of us

always squeeze each other
for music & air

communion

to worship
at the universal church
of you
      kneel at your altar
      & pray
for deliverance

murmur earthly psalms from your hymnbook
bathe your saintly feet
anoint your flesh
           in virgin oils

undo your divine buttons & bows
all your laces
& heavenly hooks

light the way
to your private chamber

        kiss your personal genesis
     adore your goddess body
taste your holy lands

awaken the congregation
within

help me rise up
     & part the sanctified gates
     of your temple

already sick of love

i want this tortured steady unbalanced
pressure twist
to find another lover

       this godforsaken ache
to walk out & drive away
here take the keys
leave & find some other romantic
to toy & tease
& tie another's heart
in sailor's knots
& have-me-nots

       when was i elected
the patron saint of lovesick pain?
forced to carry this hurtful burden
this disgrace this pity & shame
in my fixed pounding
beaten cage

a-flutter a-quiver
all my senses on fire
with the fever

of you

whisper

in my inner ear
say anything without edges

make my third eye cry

wrap your arms around me
dance your eyes
in my candlelight
dig your heels
into my electricity
hug my back
with your knees
stutter my brain & quake
my earthy hips

i want to ride your mind away
kiss it goodbye
make the walls of the world
disappear
guide me to your
lonely planet
& send me into orbit

with engine enough
to lose ourselves & gain
the galaxy

i want to fall out of the sky

& land
in your boat

sail to the heavenly edges of the earth
with you
tie all the ends together
& make a hammock
home for you

time stop space stop words stop god stop
wonder stop

        suspend everything

let the trade winds stop trading
& rock us to sleep

let the moon work its magic
& pull our tides
into one

trip to nowhere
& back

to dance inside your

ragamuffin mind
        kiss the lunatic within

somersault into your subconscious
into your tragic russian
cinema
into the eternal orbs
of your answers

the teasing wind of your id

reset our controls to zero
toss habits out the window
embrace the wisdom of our inner children
erase limits
        expand the universe
master
the impossible

        dream deep with me
lucid laughing
healing happy zulu tango dreams
dreams no one else
knows

dreams that never end

i want to know the secrets of

your hands how they dance
in the alley
speak to the blind
run through your hair
linger in mine
know how they hold a fork
& hug our spoon

wave to a friend
point direction make a sword
& slice the air
watch your hands stop time
laugh in the rain
open a door
draw hearts in the sand
knead bread
& swim to the moon

i want to know how
your heavenly hands heal
profane places
move through portals
touch the world
create new universe
folded glove snug
into mine

i don't want a perfect lover

       i need you to have faults
to balance my own

       i want to kiss your scars
your emotional wounds your
off-color tooth
your gray hairs your
sailor tongue your funny toe
your lazy eye your
off key songs

       i want to make love
to our imperfections

create an inner oil
to keep us easy

blend a cocktail of forgiveness
a foggy elixir
to take away the edges

a succulent tonic
for timeless flow

make a magic tincture of endless
desire
       fuse our flaws into days
& our days into nights
mix it all into super glue
that fixes our dreams

natural want

i want the sky & sun & sea for you
the moon & wind & night
for you

i want the earth & surf & mountains for you
the birds & whales & bears for you
the orbits & planets & comets
for you

i want the shooting stars the driving rain
the rolling thunder & the flying fish
for you

i want the fire in my belly to light up the heavens
                    for you
the ocean in my bones to swim the galaxy
                for you
the center of my axis to gently tilt endless summer
        for you

i want to give you everything good
everything true & deep & pure
everything you need & deserve
everything not bought
& sold

i want the same rain that falls on you
to fall on me to drench & quench us again
& again like me in love with you
me in love for you

you're an endless wave of atomic vibration

a powerful current that dances inside me
sweeps me away & carries me closer
surrounds me astounds me ungrounds me
drowns & washes over me in your deep
fathomless sea of oceanic impulse we
release every minuscule beat of our being
exchange massive waves & giant rolling
swells of endless cosmic drive you inside
me & me inside you we ride each other
into & through & fuse all time & space
for all time & all space for all beings
with our fluid magic molecules of love

i'm a new quaking world of

desire
        a new landscape
new shoreline new continent new
moon new planet revolving
around you
trembling all about you

an expanding universe of
wonder
radiating from you
basking in the goddess glow of you

emitting goodness & kindness
releasing unseen powers

conduit of beauty &
myth
from you into me back into you
through our silent sacred highway
of devotion

this super sub-molecular exchange
of high frequency from you

i v-v-v-v-v-vi-brate for you-u-u-u-u-u-u

my axis in wonderful wayward wobble
my once pointless mechanical orbit
now full of meaning
                & direction

my present perfect spiritual eclipse
spiraling intuitively
into you

leave your senses on high alert

i want to set off
all your alarms for love

heighten their awareness bring back
the teenage tingle
the uncontrollable shudder
your wild instinctive awakening

make you lose your inhibition to scream
anglo saxon

forget time get lost in space
in touch & sound & breathtaking
bursts of breath i want us
to embrace the immaculate lust
of holy fuck!

close your eyes to see
make your landscape ache
heave & arch to heaven

become giver & receiver

transform transport transcend
gods & goddesses
physical & spiritual right & wrong
on a quest for the holy grail
of grind i want

to give our kissing hips religion
let them deliver truth

& resurrection

i feel trapped in the labyrinth

where each aching passage
leads to the next surprising portal
through to the new no beginning
no end no exit no entrance no
orientation
yet then another more glorious door
appears & guides me to a divine
gate
of compassion into a bloom of truth
which opens to a blossom
of raging passion
into another door
after corridor
after portal after door
after gateway
that always leads me madly back
to you until i realize this
relationship
maze
is all in my mind & i am free
to forgive & love myself as much
as i choose
so now i resign myself
& choose to love you even more
deliriously caught & lost
in our everlasting loop i feel trapped

you are free to come & go

to go & come to come & let go
to come & explode to come
& scream to come & whisper
to come & quiver to come
& shake to come & glow
to come & never go to come
& be one to come & float
to come & flow to come
& sigh to come & moan to
come & laugh to come & cry
to come & come some more
with me & you & you with me
we are free & free to come & go
free to come & come & let go

fuck me

fuck me
and fuck me again
    fuck me silly
    fuck me stupid
    fuck me brainless
    fuck me painless
    fuck me out of my mind
fuck me
fuck me
and fuck me again
    fuck me here fuck me there
    fuck me later fuck me now
    fuck me into me
    fuck me into you
    fuck me into next week
    fuck my fallen angel
    fuck me back to heaven
fuck me
fuck me
and fuck me again
    fuck me till the walls fall down
    fuck me till the cows come home
    fuck me till we laugh at doubt
    fuck me till the stars burn out
    fuck my anglo inner saxon
fuck me
fuck me
and fuck me harder
    then kiss me kiss me
    touch me make me
    make me want
    and make me never
    want again

knowledge of wantless want

us holding us suspended
in wantless want
want satisfied
complete

us holding us suspended
we want unwanted want
want unwanted we

want love wrapped inside
an inner craving
ever expanding ever radiating
mystifying inspiring
cosmos
to accept perfect
imperfection

us holding us suspended
letting go of fear & doubt & pain
unwanted want we

know giving & receiving
the same spark
that ignites & lights
this great universe of desire

i always thought the world was

about losing myself in
music beauty food art drink poetry
& passion
but you you you & your unholy
divine vibrations

your hungry radiant masterful innocent naughty
pure knowing happy immaculate painful
impossible vibrations
found me

the world thinks it knows
so immense & headless
so multi-headed & fragmented
so manipulating
& power drunk business as usual
but cannot compute
our accelerating greatness
the vast karmic clout
of our humility

how we shake the foundation
of pointless norm
the worldly tail-chasing unmerry-go-round
sleeps & dreams with no idea
what we've become
dear desire

what we're going to become
even how to come
like us

you'll ruin me for life

the rest of my blissful suffering life
your smile your laugh your eyes
your mind
just the way your mind
works
          how you weave a sentence
from a few cast off symbols

how you create mood
with your tongue
from an ordinary dipthong
          a world from a pause
          a bond from a sigh

i listen to your magic
your confident sonic fabric
& picture your lips
destroying me
          leaving me in rubble
          by stairs

that no longer need
climbing

i fell asleep in the tub once asleep once

in the tub i fell asleep in the water warm
like warm tub water once asleep i fell
in shallow water deep asleep in tub water
shallow once dreams of floating & drifting
once in the tub i rubbed my belly asleep
in the deep dream tub once i fell into
another tub the other one your favorite
clawfoot one the tub you always
wanted to fall into fall asleep fall into
spring into summer i fell asleep in the tub
once i fell into the tub asleep in the water
warm like me inside your clawfoot tub
your warm your water your shallow
deep into you i always fall asleep

appointment in samsara

we first met in the middle
of rainbow bridge
three hundred feet in the sky
gazing down on otter & loon
        i guessed you were otter
        & i the diving loon
                but was it the other way
                around? we witnessed
billions of gallons
disappear under bridge
cleansing lifetimes of karma
blessing the present blessing us
        our newborn blue planet
        spinning at thousands of miles
                an hour in space with no hope
                of ever going back or slowing
down i stared into you
& tons of hardened steel girders
vibrated twisted melted
into a molten mass
        of liquid happiness running
        down my cheek nothing
                what it seemed except you
                you were perfect

i come to you in the stumbling

night drunk with rain
                    & falling wine
hat full of ancient apologies
kneeling on bended destiny

seeking your forgiveness
for my childlike selfishness
because my inner teenage ego
wants all of you all the time

even though i know you
give me more & more each
day & night you give me
the earth & verse of you

but i am the grandmaster
                    of mistake
who wants more than more
who wants to warm myself
inside your sacred fireplace

who wants retreat inside your home
discover your blanket of forgiveness
disappear & sleep off all
this artless ache

the first time i fell

a million stories into you
into soft sound slow-motion
where charges spark
electric

where tongues taste & dart
            languidly chase
                        each other around

into the ebb & flow of gentle
opening & tender
pressure

where molecules of low moan
mingle with the atoms
of dancing spirits

where arms wrap hands meander
& the rest of the world
fades into hazy
horizon

what's left of what's right

i take the strong mint
from your mouth & plant it
somewhere
south
        somewhere in the center
of your pleasure
& blow until the heart
of your heaven
heats up
        steal an ice cube from
your drink & ease it
from instep over ankle
past your calf
                        up your
                inner thigh
        into a quiver shiver
& devastating
sigh

up up up
ever so slowly
to your delicious lips
suck
        what's left of what's right
& drink all of you
into me

they say nothing contains everything

but kissing you
comes close

the chase & escape
the capture & rapture
the opening & closing
the anticipation
& elation
the depth & breath
the squeeze & release
the expansion
& contraction
the rush & flush
the taste the touch the curves the swerves
& the great galactic swirl
the silent swoon
the subtle sigh
the hello & goodbye

every instant of timeless time
the bittersweet letting go
& the forever
always wanting more
& more

everything

elevating the art of suffering

i'll teach myself the art
of suffering
& become the best in my field

learn to paint my pain
compose with open
wounds
   sculpt sorrow
   tango by myself
   dance ballet with a mournful
limp

   fully describe all 300 kinds
   of romantic misery

illustrate six volumes
on the creative madness
of melancholy

you say there are roadblocks &

i say let's build a new road
let's design
a roadless road let's walk on air
to see if we like it

& you say you have kinks
so i say we all have knots to unravel
places where desire twists
our nature
into pretzels & pours
salt in our wounds

& you say but i want to know
everything for myself
i have plans
i need to work this out
on my own

& i say what are you running from
everything comes to you
whether
you want it or not
every moment an answer

& i say remember art is process
the practice of everything
even love
even your avoidance of self
strong & persistent
as my attraction to you

i love the lines of you

the outlines & the inlines of you
the lines that show me
where you are in the world
    the lines of your smile your legs
    your back
the lines of your toes hands & nose
the lines of your eyes open
& closed
the lines of your hips the lines
of your lips
        i love the lines that come out
    of your mind
& out of your pen

i love the lines you draw & withdraw
the lines you feed me
the lines of your laughter
    i love your telephone line
& the lines you walk
i love the lines
of your shine how they radiate
& connect
with all the other lines
    i love the lines in my mind
that crave the shape
& touch & sound & thought &
gift of you

thank you for calling me into

your mind waking me up
& reviving my heart thank you for understanding
me for believing
in me
encouraging me inspiring me

thank you for helping me find
enough balance to love myself again

thank you for the wonder of your words
your art your dance your heart
your humor your mail your female
your vision your compassion your passion
your lips your love your love your
love thank you for teaching me
gratitude

thank you for kissing me back & kissing
me out of the blue

thank you for loving my skies for sharing your
air your words your laugh & always
taking me with you

thank you for being my canada my paris
my new york my big sur my private beach my
public ocean my north star & southern cross

thank you for inviting me into the home
of your open arms

only the best of you

when desire becomes so strong
it overwhelms
my sense of purpose
>   even air grows hard & dark
>   space collapses shadows
>   lengthen lungs tighten

& the overcast henchmen
of selfish love
carriers of doubt
& fear dare to appear

i could easily shut down reason
chase my tail in a thousand social
circles & choke in my own
slipknot of want

instead i muster my brighter mind
& think only the best of you
remember your intentions
generous & pure
>   how sky expands
>   clouds break hearts open
>   & stars radiate

calm unruffles my inner collar
compassion for everyone
& everything easy
as breathing

what is the price of happiness?

can you buy it for a jukebox song
beg barter & trade for it
in the marketplace
for a pocketful of paper & change

   is it the absence of wisdom
can you dance for it
jump through hoops for it
can you ache for it & make it appear
like magic out of yearning

     can you pray for it
wish for it work for it save for it
slave for it spend for it
can you pretend it doesn't exist
to make the thought of it go away

    can you not want it to get it
do you have to let it go
to make it come back
does it depend on another

    is it about feeling needed
    or the need for feeling

can you buy it with beauty
youth or old age or the absence
of memory
    are some just born lucky
    or do you make it all up
       in your mind

my need for bittersweet

such sweet irony & bitter delicacy
so much dark & starry mystery

wired for work & pleasure & duty
longing for answers & meaning

how ice & fire can quench
& inflame at the same time

how beauty in every flaw
brings desire to prayer

how your galaxy swirls the alchemy
of light & dark into my mouth

the way your hungry tongue
gives god faith again

the way your breath brings life
to my air my spirit my living ghost

o sweet bittersweet desire
just one more devastating kiss

you tattooed me with

a permanent kiss from below
left the tide of your moon on my mind
pulled me under gentle waves
until there's no letting go
or wanting to let go

you hold me there in rapture
breathe meaning into my dreamstate
shine every darkened cell
vibrate sacred space through every wall
& gradual fade of borderless blur
leading me deeper into you
& you into me

you dance every way i move
take my rhythm & give me spiritual blues
you rock me you roll me enfold me
you groove me you improve me
you wrap me overlap me
you please please please me
in rock around the clockless time

you grind my impossible peaks
into hot layabout beach
fire all my fine white sand into smooth
reflective glass
show me how to see
into the mystic mirror

you teach me how to sail
without wind fly without wings
& find everlasting home
without ever leaving
your embrace

i love the library of your mind

the high holy ceiling
of your internal structure

your random synapse order

your private molecular language
your endless rows of shelves tomes & ladders
your perfect stacks
of alphabetical nonsense
your archives of sign language
your secret wings of first editions

your permission only special collections

your unabridged volumes
your personal manuscripts of memory
your salty tongue your saintly
prayers
the vast labyrinth of your poetic
pretzel logic

i love the complete library of your mind

every second of every minute
of every hour
you invite me through
your doors

they say desire is strongest

most extreme & passionate
during the chase
when the hunt begins & animal mind
locks in
to focus on attaining
or avoiding

both choosing freedom
one to conquer one
to escape

happily ever-after
anti-climatic

but each day i chase you anew
because i want you
to want you more
& the more i want you
the more i focus
not to dominate submit or conquer
but to love

to transcend want
while never unwanting you

the spirit is in the mind the mind is

in the face the face is in the blood
the blood that flows in my body
the body that runs to you that flows
in you that never wants to leave
you that always wants to come to
you to come in you to come for you
& you to come for me to swim
in you in your blood the blood
of your face the face of your mind
the mind of the spirit that flows
into mine that flows into my mind
that flows from the spirit of
your body into mine

i don't ever want to wash you

off i don't ever want
to wash you off
i don't ever want to wash you off
i want to keep your scent
in my hair on my fingers under
my wear

i don't ever want to wash you
off i want to know you're always here
i want to taste you
everywhere
i want to touch the places
you've left your touch
on me

i want to lick the salt of our love
name all the nectars
in your garden
rediscover the honey from
your body on me
i don't ever want to
wash you off

i want to layer you on me
on & on & on me
layer after layer
drip after drop every essence
of sweat always opening
the flower
of everlasting you

if we ever get what we want

will we be satisfied or
disappointed

will one of us think i expected more

will we discover something hidden
reveal a sad dimension

will expectations lead us astray
will a turn
become a twist
a loop a loop will a loop
turn into a knot
a simple bow or feel
like a noose

will desire turn sour & curdle
        is anything ever exactly
        what you want

does the compromise in everything
create & destroy each gift

you took me to the wishing chair

& i sat at your feet
gazing up at effortless beauty
becoming one
with 300 year old mahogany
deftly carved dragon & phoenix
surrounded by windows
shrouded in cloud

my turn i sat there with you
at my feet

a woman from ethiopia remarked
how the halo on the chairback
fit my head perfectly

i wished for your eternal happiness
your peace of mind
your search for the holy
in the profane

lastly i wished for you
one day
to wish for me

climate shifts dollar shrinks

earth quakes
minds wobble
governments
crumble
bees bumble
galaxies spiral
ants revolt
letters missing
numbers
      don't add up

instincts forgotten
maps lost
religion rots
answers uncertain
faith aimless
vows lie
music fades
atoms split
hearts break
life decays

universe expands
flux flux flow
order change
disorder
fluid random flux
everything
in flux
everything
in flux

everything makes me think of you

makes me wonder where
you are what you're thinking
if you're drinking
enough water
getting enough rest
what shoes you're wearing

are your museum socks
hanging up to dry? are you eating
mother's mac & cheese?
are you drinking latte
by lenin
or overlooking the canal?

i wonder what comes next
& look at my hands
        once you kissed them
then i hug myself
& remember how fluently
form melted

i sit in my office & suddenly i'm
transported to yours
it's too damn easy
to miss you
even my keyboard reminds me
of your back

i want to teach desire to meditate

learn to breathe from deep within
stop the world & let it go

inhale goodness purpose
calmness center my imperfect universe
& exhale all the mindspring spinning
tail-chasing soul sucking
material world
agitation

i want to give you wings
to your highest tibetan dreams
help you soar from spiritual decay
& return whole
become perfect desire
mindless desire
eternal desire

i want to inhale you radiate you
& beam you back
to heaven

i can't want to want
at all

the geography of infinity

as the sun goes down i dream
of moving into your landscape

how my peninsulas fit
into your harbors

how our bays ebb & flow
our tides pool & mingle

how our continents shift together
make peaks & slowly drift apart

how everything vibrates & aches
flows shakes grows quakes

radiates & moves matter
into space that never ends

dear desire you're a stunning beast

astonishing beauty of the third
degree you tempt me
with your art
the art of temptation
hook me with your smile
land me
with your laughter

knock me out with your kisses
the kiss of life & death

lock me up with your language
the language of mystery
& madness

then throw away the key

you wear the body of a magic
pony dancer
plant enticing dreams
in my mindfield

you whisper happiness doesn't exist
even convince me your freedom
is vital to survival

how i wish i could give us
both our freedom

i want you i need you i want

you i love you i need you i want you i love you i
heart you i head you i arm you i leg you
i leg you a lot

i accept you i reject you i want you i feel you i touch you
i kiss you i miss you i don't diss you i want you i need
you i love you i heart you i need you i love you

i heart you i hear you i ear you i fear you
i know you i nose you i open you i close you
i want you you haunt me i need
you i bleed you

i row you i sail you i drive you i fly you i ride you i
show you i blow on you i lick you i taste you i play
with you i pray for you i want you i need you
i love you i love you

i like you i friend you i fiend you i wean off and on
you and come back for more because i
want you i need you i love you

i heart you i head you i arm you i don't harm you i
leg you and i leg you a lot i do i do i do you because
i love you i want you i want you i want you

i refuse to make a molehill

out of my love for you
bulldoze & steamroll our memories
our future our presents
erase our universe
without a trace

my inner strength will
bamboo bend in your gale force
knots will not snap
or stop my holy earthquakes
for you

my pulsing blue
blood for you racing around inside
as you chase a dream around
your volcano
now snowcapped & calm

comforted by millions of pines
yews fir spruce cedars hemlocks while
you recede into ice & shadow
my nonstop moon
will warm & light your path

clinging to a dream

dear desire i did not ask the cosmos
to fall in love
i did not quest or request
the joyous painful
ache of us

not on my shopping list
or things to do
not in my lucid dreams
or new year's resolutions
i never wanted to lose control
or gain the world

all i wanted was to grow up
& be myself when you taught me
how to laugh again
gave me back my dignity
made me feel awake

but now i can't sleep at the thought
of losing you no i did not ask
the cosmos for love
i did not want to hold on
& on so tight

flashback to dawn

remember when i was trying
to fall off this splintered mortal coil
by drinking too much tequila

night after night i poured myself into a stupor
beyond incoherence to hallucination
until that night the heavens opened up
dumped oceans of wind & rain
on me as i zigged zagged my way
through puddles of drunkenness
screaming your name
into the inkblot evening

pitch black & alone with pain
because i knew you too were out there
you heard my voice
both frantic & fearless

that night you talked me down
through the ether
coaxed me out of the bottle
gave me back my legs

turned ever-dark
into day

o sweet passion you hot

sweaty mistress of timeless desire
you wonderful warped distortion
of eternal love
you endless ferris wheel
marriage of relentless obsession
you raging fire
of effortless power

my holy & profane zeal for you
shakes me makes me earthquakes me
jumpstarts my electric heart
flowing into the source
of all meaning

into the blood that pumps & pulses
then radiates into the spring
of ancient spirit
& connects us all to each other

into the well that heals & makes us whole
makes us better than ourselves
remakes us in the image
of gods & goddesses throwing
thunderbolts
of our better angels

exciting & igniting the rest of
the wanting world

flashback to dusk

your wild horses race across
the sky again

      pull the golden hours
behind them
          bring the twilight of knowing
               into view

make room for moons
of forgiveness

      how i honor
          the godlike power

in the hooves of words

you weave yourself into my dreams

create the fabric of future
the clothes i wear
the skin i'm in
the thoughts i think
the sonata of your laughter
my elevator emotions my eagle wing visions
our on and off again love affair
with gravity

the threadbare strings
of the universe
playing god's stratocaster
running over the bridge of moans
to the rhythm
of sighs
your crisscross body-hugging
zigzag knit
the delicate interlace
of our interwoven world

your spin your warp
your loom

dear desire why are we so co-dependent

so dualist so together apart why
do we need each other
feed off each other

bleed into each other why
is satisfaction always just out of reach

glimpses of happiness why
only glimpses why do you send me
temptation in sensual forms

where is your filter what are your limits
sometimes you make me think

there are no limits i have fathomless
capacity for more & more
& we keep expanding into sky

to other planets & realms
we fly on comets

make rings around ourselves
holy lips kissing the great
ellipse of life

just trying to keep breathing

dear desire you're a hot
& cold smoking
gun
in my mouth

a killing field for lovers
a sex & death dance
in & out
of the human race

embracing a headless tango
too often touch & go-go
a long deep free fall from grace
our feast or famine garden

where hearts start & stop
e   x   p   a   n   d
& crash
soar & crush

& even sometimes turn to mush
o romance
so easy to inhale
so hard to resist

the perfect cigarette
burns so bright
& alive
as it kills

random relativity

o dear desire you live inside me
moved in when i was asleep
& now you're the star
of my dreams
in every cell of my being

the ease of our give & take
our breathing in sync
our craving
so willing to please
so willing to leave

so flexible & forgiving
so wanting to revolve around each other
so needing to suspend the laws
of motion physics
enough to drive newton

mad with randomness & einstein
insane with mistress jealousy
traveling in circles
as we both pass through
this massive hole

in time

how much is enough

dear desire how much ego
goes into love? how much dilutes
passion or poisons the truth?

is ego even necessary? does it get
in the way or add spice? give tension?
heighten action? play off drama
for energy?

will ego win out? can it be stopped
before it takes over?

how much ego does true love require?
is there a universal recipe? does it depend
on the love or the lover?

how much stroking insecurity?
how much not enough? how much
too much? how much stoking
keeps the fire alive?
does desire even know

about love

conviction

dear desire you come
as close to perfection as possible
even your imperfections
bring me to my knees

perhaps you're perfection
in disguise

maybe if you appeared too perfect
you'd seem unattainable
unbelievable
& i'd feel unworthy

you balance the sacred
& profane

find the spirit in every detail
you feed me fuel me
drive me
make me want to live & die

center me with calm

& take me to the third eye
of your storm

dear desire it's been years since

we last met & i can't
remember what you look like

all the pictures in my mind
even the private images
you sent
the ones too painful to view

are lies

i've almost forgotten the sound
of your voice
the taste of your lips

the way we worked up a sweat
morning
noon & night

you let go so long ago

i can't remember
if you were once real
or if
i made you
up

from the start

i create you as much as

you create me
but dear desire when you
push me away
a massive vacuum
attacks
my chest

until i feel so small
i don't have the strength
to push pen
across
scrap paper

as if my life suddenly becomes
one meaningless doodle
in space

all our sacred words
written in invisible ink

i roll into a ball & cramp
immortality ha!
my spirit my love
stuck under
the weightless wait
of your shiny giant black
55 eyelet
hard soul boot

plot thickening

dear desire i know you can't help
being so powerful

how you rule the universe
is beyond me

the quantum mechanics
of how you put everything

in perfect motion with greed
& lust & subatomic want

the simple physics
of attraction & repulsion

the pure revolution
of particle orbit

with effortless ease
& economy of emotion

you inspire me to reduce myself
edit my needs

numb with admiration
i plot against my will

i want to want less

& more at the same time
dear desire i want to want the nothing
& everything of you

i want to drink from the magic rill
of your deepest forest

spin in your slipstream swirl
flow in your glowing
blue waves
get lost in the eddy galaxy ocean
of your pulsing stardust
tango

i want to howl at the beauty
of your liquid beast
embrace the power of your tide
take me away in deep currents
of kisses

i want to travel everywhere
& nowhere & always wake up
next to you

i want to want less & more
of you all the time

two steps forward three steps back

four steps sideways five steps
down six steps
up seven steps down
eight steps under nine steps above
three steps beyond two
steps back

seems i'm always looping forward
into the past
& i want more than
i have
yet have more than i need

my fathomless well of joy
& pain my bucketful of question marks
my steel drum of happiness
my bushel of smiles
my dark pints of forgetfulness
my peck of kisses my imperial gallon
of ocean my schooner of promise
my handful of thimbles

material measures looping forward
into the past
& i want more than
i have
yet have more than i need

dear desire if i fail

to reach you
it won't be
for lack of trying
or because i got scared
& disappeared
afraid of commitment
or break-up
or wanted my freedom
in another kind
of prison

dear desire thank you for being

my lover & teacher for wanting me as much as i want you
thank you for letting go & never giving up
for holding on to letting go
thank you for tearing me down & building me up
over & over again

thank you for being my church & home my ocean & sky
thank you for your sun & moon your face & voice
your laughter & daughter & shine
thank you for letting me brush your hair & massage
your feet cook you dinner & pour the wine

thank you for making me so grateful thank you for no end
to the thank yous i want to give you

thank you for lending me an ear thank you for the taste
smell touch & voice of you thank you for the lost & found
faded & fresh near & far real & imagined
memories of you thank you for the eternal now of you

thank you for sending me your pictures words poetry
& prayers your books post cards envelopes packages & even
the air from your jail

thank you for always thinking the best of me for always
being my friend through thick & thin again & again
thank you for taking me with you thank you for your time
& mind & your mindlessness & timelessness
your collective unconscious your constant belief in me

thank you for the silver bullet through my heart the cross
on the hill your ever-present humor the weak at your knees
the homeless at heart the wishing chair the office couch
the glass of water the myth of freedom the forgotten
movie our walks in the park & the massive
phone bill

thank you for the universe of you the whirling twirling
swirling unfolding deathless dance
of you

decades of yearning

dear desire am i dreaming you
or are you dreaming me?

sometimes i dream
      we're dreaming each other

our dreams the same dream
teaching us how to dream ourselves

how to move into the singularity
of one inclusive dream

to learn yearning is dreaming
to be now for the other

dear desire i want a peace treaty

for my tug of war
with you

i want to discover a vaccine
for jealousy & inoculate myself
with you

i want to negotiate a lasting trust
a freedom from obsession

sign on the dotted line
& disappear
with you

get lost in magnetic fields
of massive attraction

it's been so long since

we last made love i might not
know
if your tongue
will still chase mine
or even remember the way
your tender nibble awakens my animal
or how you arch to bridge skyward
& point your pouty beauty
at my ravenous lips

o the last time we danced
you didn't call out my name
or even mention
if we'd ever meet again

so in my restless mind
your soft glowing body is a vibrating
blur
& i might not recall
that dark mole
on your left shoulder
the strength of your back

or even the heat & drench
of our singing electric bodies
dripping & smacking
in sweat of ardor

our inspiration for action

our spark our key our on & offspring from shallows
of selfish to deepest spiritual hunger o desire
o creator inventor obsessor mentor

winner loser addict aggressor father mother lover
player worker we all want you & we want you
more & more

we want to flood ourselves with you drown
in your whirlpool of want o dear desire o dear immortal
muse how you master & amuse us to death

how you live a million lives promise us pleasure
& deliver us pain o how we embrace our measureless
emotional self-important suffering

how we willingly give you everything in return
time after time o dear o desire o when when when
can i see you again?

you warned me from the beginning

you said one of us
would sandcastle crumble
before the first autumn frost

you said the tides would soon wash away
all the magical evidence
of us
our moons would spin
in opposite orbit

you warned me & i believed
in you
but i never believed that

because i knew you could
do anything you wanted

you can have everything

for your birthday anything
you want just say the word hum it
chant it

send the vibration within & without
around your mountain your park
your paradise

throw a silent party
for the massive quiet inside
blow candles cut cake

expand your spirit embrace the world
& bask in the holy marvel
of universal nothing

dwell in the great void of not doing
make a few wishes for happiness
in emptiness

know everything will come to you
dear desire when you give
yourself to yourself

your murmurs still echo

echo echo echo echo echo
in my limitless ache for you

      my dreams still vibrate
      with kisses & colors

your lines still etched in
my waking mind

when i think of making plans
                i think of you
when i think of making art
          i think of you
when i think of making love
i think of you

you you you you you you you
& the path to the door that opens

      to the road that leads to
      the river of forgiveness

you told me to move into my sunshine

so i took to the deck
camped out with pen & paper
& books made in canada
full of thoughts
only canadians have

i daydreamed of moving north again

my compass points in that direction
when i think of
expansive happiness
because when desire bumps
into me in canada
she says sorry
& then we make love inside a sunset
in a blanket on a log on a beach
in the park

but not before i pour the end
of the wine
into the rising tide
& move
with my books & your landscape
into my sunshine
to canada

odd human concept control

implies fear of future
a need to restrict & constrict
an insecurity about the unknown
limits possibility

inhibits wonder exploration
risk-taking inhibition
discovery & love

dulls imagination feeds ego
offers false security
& always ends up controlling
the controller

control is out of control
orders & makes demands
wants answers definitions names
grammar
regulations hierarchy
seeks power over others
builds dams & walls
cuts things down blows things up
kills without knowing
without asking

creates brutal order

closes down the natural flow
misunderstands the beauty of chaos
& desire o dear o dear desire
how i love your freedom
from control

they say nothing lasts

eventually
everything falls apart

planets families marriages bodies cars
skyscrapers mountains molecules
atoms quarks myth & truth
everything
except you dear desire

yet i keep falling apart for you
& coming back together & no one
knows what keeps us composed
perhaps it's our apartness

unless we take a number save the date
make the effort we hardly see each other
anymore
yet when we do
the world dissolves away

buildings crumble mountains fall stars implode
atoms of you pass through me
transform into something greater
& everything we're in or on
will fall apart
like that
become something else
something less
finding a way to stay pure
stay away & together
become better

become us

humans hard-wired for want

believe if something is good
then more
must be better

until enough is exceeded
& too much attained
then obsession
addiction & never enough
never satiated never satisfied
gluttonous cycle
that wears out psyche
& wears down body
always in search
of something it thinks it wants
to destroy itself

but o desire you are different
you transform want
from death trap
to spirit that inspires
takes my hand into
your mouth

even a little
of you
is enough
to rewrite the future

it's too easy to love someone

you don't know so well
someone easy on the eyes someone
who pays you compliments
likes your art your shoes
your humor your style your timing
showers you with intermittent affection
listens to your stories
                    kisses you back
wants to walk with you
says take me to canada!
smiles when we meet
makes art makes her life art
asks for an arm wrestle
plays chess in the sunshine with you
invites you into her shower
lets you touch her
anywhere
                    everywhere
whisper poems into
her ear
trace the lines of her back
yes it's easy to love someone
you always want
to know better

on the trail of your scent

you smell of wind in sails
of birds in flight of the moon
in orbit of soil just turned
                    of clouds at dawn
            of sunshine in fall of
        that temple in tibet
my cave in india of mountaintops
in heaven of laughter
at the theatre
        of coconuts by the sea of
                butterflies on dew of whales
                    whispering to you
of popcorn for dinner of
        symphonies in vienna
                of gardenias in the jungle
                        & forest before rain
                of forgiveness to yourself
        of non-attachment to others
of an envelope from anarctica
an epic journey to the beginning
of the end of time
                of kisses in foreign showers of
            nothing to live up to but tides
pulling us ever closer

don't speak to me of wounds & open

sores & heartache & toothache & aching
backs & sore knees & cold sores & full
moons & full moans & belgian chocolate
& oysters & wine & money & masks &
medication & meditation & latte grandes
& student loans & loneliness & dandelions
& marriage & freedom & children &
nirvana & exposed nerves & exes & Os &
kisses withheld no no dear desire don't speak
unless you want to go deeper than want
don't speak unless you're ready to fly

we are animals in the desert

in the forest in the ocean
on the mountain
on the ice
in the country in
the city

we are animals wanting blood
& lust & more &
more

when our instinct kicks in
when words & future
& philosophy & religion & politics &
money & science & psychology & insecurity
& drugs & lawyers & doctors & sailors
& gurus
don't get in the way

we're wild & free

sublime radiant perfect
ancient ageless animals
in heat

wanting it
wanting want

i am the ghost of you &

you the ghost of me
perfect shadowless & longing
for imperfection
                    wanting human

questing for answers & flesh
regressing to womb
before we had face before
fingers & toes

            before id before sex
            before names before light

swimming in mother's soup
plasmic ghost in the machine

now we want to return
to the magic gift
of vibrational spirit
                    without need

without food shelter clothing
without status passports & law

before anything mattered
before borders lines & other
before separation
                    before fall

you left me with dozens of

perfect memories instants
when clocks stopped & we made
love to eternal now

you left me
thousands millions gazillions
& they play on a continuous reel
in my head
a loop of forever
one memory at a time

as if you were always receiving
& beaming bliss
radiating your own sun
one hundred years ago to hundreds
of years
in the future

     so many accordion instants

expanding & contracting
within & without
physics

dear desire you wear the mask

of happiness well
almost fits
when you're not running away
from yourself

but you know you can't
win that race
without losing everything first

the void so inviting
we can't stop ourselves
until i don the mask of death
to cheat on myself

on & on we run
as the road gets longer

the faster we go
the further away from each other
we become

our loophole in illusion
complete

location location location

dear desire when i asked
for your address you made
something up

i spent hours looking for you
which made me laugh
at how easily you evaded me

later you sent me exact directions
even left a note on your door
to come on in

we kissed to the same song
for 35 minutes until i told you
we were stuck on replay

but so were our lips & tongues
until you changed the music
& our clothes came off

then we made an impression
your bed
still remembers

patron saint of more & less

dear desire you're so beautiful
you can never die
no matter what happens
you will live on in books
photos movies
memories & dreams

whenever mortals want more
or fall into wonder trouble or love
you'll be there
to comfort the afflicted
elevate their lust
infect their passion

inject yourself into their blood
morph flesh & faces
change identities
move into new jobs homes
clothes countries & states
of mystic mind

o dear desire the patron saint
of more & less
bless us
with your illusions
free us from perfection
& insignificance

you can't write an equation

to open a heart
follow a lucid sequence
to win her hand
add up the truth to get
her into bed

there's no logic in love
nothing to count on
not even gravity
especially not time
matter expands transforms

into ether
melts & mixes molecules
to attract dissolve
& fuse
become each other
greater power

until they're blue in the face
like hindu gods
avatars & noodle soup
cotton candy clouds
ice & fire

marooned in marriage

this bed tonight is the same
as last night
& the night before last & on & on always
the same
ocean of emptiness
without you

        i toss & turn the waves roll
tides take covers away
pillows wash in
& ebb out
        i don't know who
        i'm sleeping with
        anymore

we never touch
not even by accident
there's nothing to say except
turn off the light
& whatever

while you exist on
another plane
        14 hours away

i am in room 1414
& have
no idea what that means
except

i miss you

if i don't want something it doesn't matter

how low the price how easy to get what
it's worth how much he she or it wants me
but if i want something i won't weigh risks
price is no object i become focused & fixed
throw wisdom & patience & restraint out
the window unbound by earthly chains
my world is just desire & me & we wrestle
until both of us win until matter & spirit
are one until flesh falls from the bone
until decay has no more work & everything
broken down until we both realize there
was never anything there to begin with
nothing but want on a limb but o what
beautiful limbs & o what a way to go

sometimes waiting is action

dear desire i met a woman at the night bazaar
who read my tarot cards about you
& she said beware

blood pressure & stomach problems
one of us might need an operation
but by the end of the year
all will be well
job health
& love

we can make a fresh start because she said
all obstacles are in the head

then picked up the star card
told me
this card trumps all the others
even the hanging man
the devil
& the king of wands

fame & fortune & happiness & love
are all upon the horizon all within reach
at the end of the year

just like you said before you left
let everything come to you
let everything come
to you

my mind is on a loop for you

futile as it sounds futile as it sounds
futile as it sounds
you're in another realm
i'm here & now
you're there & how
who knows when or if yet
   my mind is on a loop for you
   my mind is on a loop for you
not her or him or her not her or him or her
not her or him or her
or all those others you think i'd rather
instead my mind is on a loop for you
my mind is on a loop for you
     wounded hurt & blind
     wounded hurt & blind
     wounded hurt & blind
you tell me nevermind
i'll gladly forget for a price
but how does this movie end
with a whimper or a bang
or a satisfied sigh
   my mind is on a loop for you
   my mind is on a loop for you
this beautiful loop of sighs
looping in my mind
for you
looping in my mind
for you
   on a loop that never dies

remember the morning i woke suddenly

& hugged you as if i could
squeeze all the love out of your body
                    into mine

you called me a koala bear
because i didn't want
                      to let go

but life is about letting go
so i drove off into the sunrise

left you to sleep in your car as i slipped
between cold home sheets
          in a frigid bed

i dreamt we booked a flight
               to tibet
         & you said

i hope you never
fall
                    in love
with a married woman

hooked on desire

a friend of mine said you
have daddy issues
      another friend said it sounds like
      she's pulling away
a little birdie told me stay
strong have faith
         the cat down the lane said
         you're a handful you're trouble
the lost puppy dog in me
wants to please
      the rogue in me thinks
      every woman has her charms
the realist in me says
plenty of fish in the sea
        but you dear desire
      are the fish that hooked me
so when i fantasize
i dream of you landing me
      praising me braising me
      but first feeding me
more line as i swim
            further out
      to sea

dear desire i want to shave myself

closer & closer to you
lather my mind
& lop off a few layers

these prickly whiskers of want
grow a little everyday & everyday

                    i cut them as close as
              five blades allow
          then wonder why do i bother
to spend time & money
for smoothness

am i a slave to marketing
& the best a man can get

do i do what i do only to
invite a softer smoother face
to snuggle next to mine

i practice for the day you
come near enough to see if
my razor still has an edge

if only i could shave time
or half my longing
for you

into our lofty mire

after we both knocked
each other
off our pedestals

we felt more at ease

twice felled fallen angels
wings clipped
halos dimmed
our bleeding hearts
pouring out
into rain

nowhere on earth to go
but up

now we know
most of the time
we must fall
down

to get there

my heart flutters between

the universal & the so-so
subatomic
it won't be divided

i'm a trillion billion yo-yos
at the end of my string

your hand waves hello your hand
waves goodbye your hand
waves hello

& i'm spinning faster than
around the world

over the falls walk the dog
rock the cradle
                    i gaze at god
          in the mirror
your face inside the looking glass
looking back at me

gives me reason to breathe
to survive these up & down days
that fall to pieces

& eventually come
together

you take me to the place where

holding is letting go where
leaving is arriving
& arriving
is gone

where a kiss is lost until we part
find our lips lost in alone

where laughter is symphony
& a smile worth
small fortune
where walking is flying & flying
is breathing & breathing is
tasting your air

where art is everything
& everything is art & the art
of everything falls apart
in an artful way

where love never ages
& you drape yourself over me

where legs tangle
& toes mingle & everyday
new language born

dear desire i love the place your eyebrow

stops the curve of your calf
  the strength
of your back
  the length of your toes
    the shape of your hands
  the taste
of your mouth
  the shine of your smile
    the step of your gait
  the veins
in your temple
  the string of your hair
  the music
of your laughter
  the mole on your shoulder
    the lines on your cheeks
  the angels
of your presence
  the confidence
of your lips
  the dart of your tongue
  the warmth of your body
  the field
of your holy
  the compassion of your heart
  the answer
in your eyes
  the beauty that surrounds you
  the place you stand
i love

every poem a love poem

a prayer for you a wanting
a wish a virgin sky
                              a secluded clue
an empty mind a new beginning
beginning anew
an old theme all for you

even the twisted & wicked lines
disguised as fuses
for love bomb bursting dams
making rivers of hot blood
pumping rapids
of passion all for you

my every thought a love poem
rushing over rocks round bends
under bridges
shape-scaping new words
new worlds new
wordless
worlds all for you

in the cemetery

you said the reasons
for death are
                as limitless
as the reasons for life

then kissed me again & again
filled me up with both

life & death

whereabouts unknown

dear desire you must be by now
beyond suffering beyond yourself
beyond influence

beyond emotion beyond perfection
beyond performance beyond satisfaction
beyond weather

beyond success beyond judgment
beyond mountains beyond beach
beyond money beyond god

i imagine you ceased becoming
you've already learned to be
simple & deep & empty

pure blue sky
dreamless
dream

it always comes back to you

dear desire seems everything
always begins & ends with you
your motivation
       your reception
           your perception your
                connection

your affection your inflection
      your rejection your
detection your selection
your dissection your direction
your misdirection your insurrection
your resurrection
our it
the inner it of it

how it effects infects
& accepts the whole of it it it

          the it of it
        the it of you you the it of me me
        the it of us
   it
   always comes
back to you & me me

everything's breaking up

the whole material illusion
splitting apart &
dissolving
opening up lifting off
relationship going going gone

into & through loopholes
rabbit holes
wormholes
black holes white holes
& holy portals of

om

in & out & roundabout
on & under & over
& out
breaking down breaking up
breaking through

splitting   apart & breaking on
evolving dissolving
unresolving
our whole reationship gone
breaking up & long long gone

i'll never forget your performance

our only spring at the beach
overlooking the bay where one day
i hope you'll scatter my ashes

we sat on sand among stray logs
reading obscure books & drinking coffee
from to-go cups
when you pulled a feather from your jacket
another & another & then a knife
so you ripped into the non-rip material
removing handfuls of down

releasing white fluff up watching it
fly again
returning it back to the wind
back to magical updrafts
into clouds of compassion
as each feather landed
on pages of words written for another
in coffee cups poured for another
on faces & hair & sweaters & sand
even some floating farther away
into the brine of the bay

until your jacket became a metaphor
of death & resurrection

now an empty shell without a soul
you said goodbye & buried it in green dumpster
behind the oceanside apartments
the first place in vancouver
i ever lived

right before the first time we met

you said let's pretend
we don't know anything about
each other
let's start over

but i wear my scars on my sleeve
& found it hard to block out
all my cuts & burns
from your tongue & fire

so i was excited & scared
to take off my armor
hand you my weapons
& surrender

my powerless power
fall to my knees
close my eyes lose every excuse
& hope to die

i promised myself i wouldn't let you hurt me

wouldn't suffer under your spell
i'd try to teach myself
to touch & not lose touch
fall & not fall apart
love & let go

dear desire i promised myself
i could resist you when i needed to
when you needed me
to untangle
our complicated knots
find the ends & loop them
through somehow
absorb absolve

dissolve the parts of you
that melted into me
stop these longing vibrations
from expanding me & sounding
so lonely feeling so hollow
painting me so blue
from the inside

ha!

i might as well try to stop the universe
from birth

natural grace

when i keep my life simple
breathe in breathe out
my life becomes
simple

when i make my life peaceful
one breath calm one compassion
my life becomes
peaceful

when i fill my life with love
kissed by sun hugged by cloud
my life becomes
full of love

when i walk with you dear desire
one step here one step now
we touch the earth
& let it go

turns out you're the mountain not me

you walk around yourself
seek lower vibration
alone

you've already been to the top
reached your peak

took others there but now you solo
find the trails around
the base of you

kiss the ground with your body
reach deep inside yourself

reach beyond wanting
deeper & deeper into
inner space

touch the happiness of emptiness
embrace the void & know

everything evaporates
as if you & your mountain
were never here

the mountain loses itself in itself

desire lost & found in desire
every want each ache & crave

wish by wish particle by particle
element by element molecule

by molecule tumbles into gravity
wobbles & stumbles

falters & totters until a stream
of super consciousness

expands & contracts & expands
& flows downhill from one to another

into the mountains of the dissolved
into flesh into beach into sea

we sift ourselves
your mountain & my coast

between the smallest grains
of warmest wantless sand

never be

dear desire
i'll never be good

enough
if i continue

to hold on to this
foolish notion

that i'll never be
good enough

most seem drawn to excitement

they dream to reach the highs & lows
of their rollercoaster psyches

the thrill of speed the g-force liftoff
the freefall of splashdown
the instant before they leap from airplanes
the adventure of questing
& epic tail-chasing

all the aimless ego butterfly flirting
with hundreds of fragrant flowers

the hunt & chase & the capture & kill
over & over until
there's no time to savour

but o desire you bring helium smiles
to this punch drunk round-a-bout
gently lift everything near you
levitate my understanding
slow down my impatient electrons
stop my inner chaos & decay
make me want less
of anything else
except your mountain calm

you watch over me
wake me bathe me in shade & light
balance me ground me to gravity
& eternity
grant me grace & flow

go slow you said & i thought

of all the times in my life
they drove me
with carrot & switch
told me to speed it up or go faster
work harder get more make more finish first
push push push yourself!

do better do better than your best
work harder pick up the pace
go faster faster
not good enough
push it push it move it!
don't dawdle

you're better than that
get going be fast be first
push push yourself
get out in front & stay there
work harder finish first
go faster go faster go faster!

but only you said go slow
only you knew i needed to hear
g o   s l o w
you knew how to squeeze
an hour from a second
& make a kiss

last

forever

there's always a catch

easy to let go of work
easy to let go of furniture
easy to let go of china
easy to let go of appliances
& conveniences

easy to let go of the car
easy to let go of knickknacks & paddiwhacks
easy to let go of accumulation
location & expectation

easy to let go of the booze
& too much food
easy to let go of excess
triple X & the ex-wife
easy to let go of heartache mind games
& power trips
dead ends & happy endings
fear & lust
fashion & bacon
& old time religion

easy to let go of the struggle for survival
the sirens of chocolate & caffeine
& lady nicotine

easy to let go of ugly & beauty
even easy to let go of my clever mutating
know-it-all ego
but so hard too hard so hard
to let go of you

come here come on come over

dear desire come here
come on come
over here
                    what are you
doing where are you
who are you
come here come on
come over here
                    where are you
come here come on
where are you
come closer
(i want to tell you a secret)
come on come over
here come come come
on & on & on
                    come here
what a world what
a come on
over here where are you
what are you doing
come on come
                    over here
where are you
what a world come over here
come here ever
closer
                    come on i want
i want i want
to tell you come on
come here ever closer
ever closer forever
                    further away

everything whirls at the speed of light

the second time we visited
my church my garden
                    my green

i took you to the poet's grave at sunset
& you finger-painted the stone
            of her cheeks

with water from the grotto
while our falling star
                        bathed us
                        in orange glow

lighting up the timeless beauty
            of your bones

then we walked slowly downhill
to third beach to watch
                    god paint the sky
            with a palette
of primaries

each moment mixing in more red
until the tide kissed
            our toes
                        & violet waves
swirled
        in our eyes

the last known photo of desire

looks exactly like you
       your eyes & hair your pout
       legs lips & skin

she comes across with attitude
& spark
as if she wants to be loved by a few
yet wants the whole world
to want her
       birds bears butterflies
       & bees
       play around her
flowers become her halos
mosquitoes sing her
lullabies
       trees fly from afar
       to witness
       her mountains
       move around her fog
       & dance in her haze

her aviator glasses glow
like insect specs
in that last snapshot

flash of you

the goddess of love & suffering

you breathe life into the lungs
of the lonely
give wings to the beaten & broken
make sand understand

it was once a mountain

dear desire o dear you blinded me
with want & beauty

i ate my own bait
swallowed my own hook
forever lodged deep in my ego
which doesn't want
to let go
doesn't want to know
in a world of catch & release
better to give than receive

in this grand illusion of perpetual dissolve

i flip & flop & mask my gasps
for love & holy holy holy
suffering

haiku blues

dear desire
i am the mad puppetmaster
of my own pain

special delivery

dear desire i want to slip into
an envelope & come
in your mailbox

lesson from the quiet

after hours of hours & dozens of switchbacks
ups & downs & ups & downs
i met desire
where the air thins enough
to pucker a water bottle
& the loud quiet of mountain meadow
explodes into a wildflower opera
all blooming & dying
for each other

vibrant waves of color ricochet
off sky off eyes off the whole range of peaks
& valleys surrounding us
as we sat by the trail feasting
on the juicy flesh
of soft peaches & perfect plums

windless & birdless
we listened to the awesome quiet
tasting & soaking in stillness

quiet so quiet a shower of three pine needles
roared like a storm in the night
before a small pinecone hit ground
& hand grenade waves shook the earth

later when i lost the moment
on a rant about teenage wasteland
hours from internet & shopping malls
a stone's throw from tahoma's peak
you whispered

i don't hear the mountain
complain

when we met on the mountain top

you read from the book
of pilgrim
then showed me how to wrestle the wild
from my inner beast

we howled into the wind

our animal sounds blew back to us
while raptors flew

        sideways

you sliced cheddar with your driver's license
as the air turned to wine & filled us
with bravado

surrounding pines crackled with life

contagious waving boughs
of wonderful welcome

all the islands floating at our feet

we kissed the future
into each other

you are nearsighted dear desire

but you also help me
see things
that aren't fully there

you are my lighthouse my campfire
my headlamp my mountaintop
night sky full
of endless ember stars

you illuminate everything good
& draw me into your flame
into that deepest spark

of undying heart

union man

i'm nothing but a love factory
making love for you
making love making love making love
in everything i do
wheels turning karma's burning
pistons pumping turning nothing
into something
that makes everything i do

making love making love making love
a labor of love to fill the void
with love
making love
i'm nothing but a love factory
making love for you
making love making love making
love in everything i do
making tender words & blissful moans
with a healing touch
that sails me around the world
to bring you home

i'm nothing but a love factory
making love for you
making miles of smiles & everafter laughter
making a happy tongue not a gun
on your trigger
making love making love making love
to take away the space
that keeps us apart
stop the clock & open your heart
i'm a union man all the way

'cause i'm making love making love
making love in a love factory
i'm making love making
love from me to you
making love in my love factory
& i love my job making love to you
making love making love making love
in everything i do

a stone called desire

over a bridge in the big city
there's a museum full of stones
        you take me there because
        the stones have magic
        they speak a secret language

some balance on air like birds
while others grow out of ground
like trees like crops
        some meditate on density
        some hang themselves & bleed
        like icons from the inside
others blend into each other
fuse & tell stories
like ancient totem poles

a stone called desire tells me
in another country & time
        you will build
        two writer's shacks in a field
        with wheels & sails
catch each summer breeze
gently bump our words
& bodies
into each other

as seasons change
        replace wheels
                with sled slides she said
                                we'll race madly
        across frozen cornfields
& dream our own
magic stones

desire runs a cinema

where continuous movies
play on the big screen

action drama comedy sci-fi & horror
all walk by

her eyes director & editor

the parade of characters endless
every face a script
written on it

the smell of popcorn lingers
in her hair

wherever she sits
the world passes by

that unmatched autumn morning you

took me on a picnic
to mount pleasant cemetery
we sat under
a century old cherry tree
gnarled & wizened from 400 seasons
in every kind of weather

noshed on small curds & cantaloupe
at the head of william best
who passed in 1926

then we reclined resting our bones
with thousands of others
hanging onto gravity
& the last threads of our mortal
relationship
cloud watching
with an ear for the tweets
of lost hummingbirds

     all of us
spinning 900 miles an hour
through space

the long kiss goodbye started with

a few empty nervous words
& a moment of retreat
                    then
            a slow cautious glide
until my lips found
a match
        my hands touched your face
        your hair your ear

our tongues teased each other

me inhaling your breath
wanting to suck all of you up
        my hand losing grip using gravity
        to follow your curves
                to the crossroads
of heaven & thighs
        slipping under your dress
        between folds of time

my always hungry lips whispering
i love you i want you i love your forever
over & over in a cascading loop
of everlasting
                vibration

we stayed in that suspended state
20 minutes
20 years
20 centuries
            20
        scores
of scores

when you disappear & leave

me alone to flounder
in the low tides of my imagination
i lose my sense of purpose
my bearings my rudder
my holy compass
dear desire i

become directionless deflated
jelly soft & spineless
i drift
        drift
                drift aimlessly
with each new wave
same as the next wave
same as the next wave
stuck in moment after moment
of hollow dreams
lost plans
blank gray slates
infinite corridors & empty
stairwells of wrong
turns & dead ends

i practice patience & letting go
especially ego
but doubt slips in
offers me an anchor of heartless charms
& tempts me again & again

to follow her
down

fitting room

we discover new ways
to fit together

our life-size puzzle of arms & legs
hearts & heads fingers & toes
merge & fall into another
mingle & tangle
in perfect tango

our parts welcome each other
instinctively believe
they belong together

each bit finds space & piece
& peace & skin
becomes a perfect part
of the whole

a spoon a hug a kiss in bed
in car on rug on train in air on walk
on water
in rocking chair

when were we measured dear desire
coincidence or kismet?
who cares

with you
i am unpuzzled

even when you push me away

don't kiss me back or threaten
to move to
         wherever

even when you don't return my email
evade questions
or disappear for days
even when you make fun of my language
fashion haircut accent lack
of song memory
or breath

even when you say i don't love you
but i could love you

o dear desire even when you break off
little pieces
      of my heart & leave them
behind
for the dogs & birds
in the park
it doesn't seem to matter
      because there's no end to you
      in me no place where
      my thoughts of you stop

you're the bell that keeps ringing
expanding the circle inside me

        you're the clock stopper
     the fire starter the elevator
to everything holy

dear desire my heart sutra for you

so full of hurt & happiness
so perfect in want
so imperfect in love
     so impossible to get close
     so impossible to get away
so open & accepting
so prickly & embraceable

days without you
become mountains & hours with you
endless dreams
     each running into the other
     colliding & smashing all
the boring bits
to smatters of smithereens

raining a deluge of craving
a million elephants of memories
encyclopedias of passion
     an everlasting longing
     for lover's hunger
leaving oceans of emotion
floating in the lost ghost of gravity

all senses lead to dissatisfaction

expectation can & will be used
against me & you dear desire
are everything & nothing

> you show us
> how the universe works

you perpetuate the laws
of attraction & rejection
selection & connection

> how effortlessly
> you thread the needle

move us through the eye
& weave us
into your magic fabric

> you teach us songs
> to seduce our pains

you sing us into our dreams
where everything seems
a perfect means to an end

how big my heart how elastic

this blood pumping universe
how often can it expand & contract before
meeting its match
          & break

      does a heart have memory
      can it touch the future
      kiss the past again & again
can it fill itself with tenderness
then suddenly turn hard
              sharp & black

      when it melts does it disappear
      can you lose a heart
      like you can lose your head
can you retool another like a new set of keys
is the heart where love is kept
or hidden or
           discovered

      & how far can it open
      does a broken heart grow roots
      fade away or scatter seeds
where do tears go when a heart cries
why dear desire does my heart
cry out
      for more?

our lady of perpetual heartache

of superior sweet & bitter
torture
of everlasting
longing of eternal seduction
& unfulfilled lust
o dear desire your relentless virus
invades new territory
penetrates deeper
every minute every day
every week my weakness
my inner man
further reduced to child
simpering & helpless
my once godlike
clay
cracked & crumbled
into common dust
left without even ruin
to admire
   not even a memory of want
    worth clinging to
only the slightest hint
of shark shaped
shadows
moving slowly through
the hollow halls
of temptation & darkness

breaking in two

that was a good fight you said
8 out of 10 you said

i replied is it a good fight
when you land
           all the punches?

o you know dear desire
everything isn't a struggle for control
a serious game of who's on top
an arm wrestle for dignity
a duel of egos & authenticity
or who can draw
           first blood

to break each other's dreams
& will & heart & bank & lust &
crash two trains of thought
                head on
our big horned battering rams
knocking each other
              senseless
why do i always end up
apologizing
          to prove
you're always right?

the art of mistake redux

when you tell me art helps us
love each other
i begin to understand
          why you taunt & tease
          & bring out the best & worst
in me

o dear desire
how i loathe the worst in me

especially when exposed
to you & the further
                              i fall
& fall   apart
the more artless i become

& i wonder what have i become
          what has want wrought
          but more want

& i sting myself
with barbs inside me
until everything inflated
          ego pride love
          happiness
          all punctured & flat

happy new year

we never recovered from the night
you left our bed
                    for the couch

            & all the drama that ensued
            merely punctuation

for the sound of egos clashing
& blazing lust melting down

            the threats & anglo saxon epitaphs
            the stomping & storming

the knife throwing the silent treatment
the running away

                    mostly the running away
            cold ashes

dashed dreams

we shed our skin

& looked within a mirror
reflecting past
behold! the mountain
in a grain of sand

your pearl so perfect
& perfectly imperfect
my shell so hard & sharp
glad fortress of failure

what happens when
two lovers afraid
            of each other
want the same thing

what happens when
longing
becomes the object
of yearning

limbo

the plucking & playing
     & pulling & thumping & beating
         of broken heart strings

        the pressing & tapping & poking
     pushing & shoving of hot
& cold buttons

the constant looping & tangling
& tying & raveling & untying
of emotional knots
the slack untuned random
relentless heavy flapping flapping
of saturated relationship sails

o dear desire our psychic tug-of-war
     this zero sum carnival game
         no picnic in the park

       neither getting what we want
    yet not willing to give in
& fully let go

stalemate

the first time we played chess
our spleens fused
into each other into glorious spring
sunshine into blooming
flower exuberance
into the sweet
deck air
of the coffee shop
by the canal
where you wore
cool blue flip flops
with hot orange corduroys
& even though
i captured most of your men
                    you were clever enough
                          to surprise me
                            with a draw
                              but now
                          dear desire
                    the game is cutthroat
        & you've taken piece after piece
                        of my heart
                    until i'm playing
                          by myself
                & i don't know why
        i let you capture anything
                that still belongs
                            to me

the unknowing

i miss your chameleon face
how you change from radiant
to black & blue to green
& back to you

your shape shifting ways
from bunny to tiger
pig to bird fox to toad & horse
to breathtaking moon

your clothes your diet your art
the way you move through
the hungry soup of us stirring the pot
adding new spice

dear desire i've never
been closer yet felt further away
from knowing
who you really are

dear desire how you hound

my memories
how i dog myself with tail-chasing
& running in my dreams

how i hope you'll call my name
whistle me home
bring me treats
rub my belly
teach me new tricks
& run your nails up & down
my back

how much i want to please you
chase away dark shadows
protect you
from your fears
keep the postman at bay
be there for you always walk
by your side
warm you at night

how i long to smell your human
curl around your tail
lick your face
& taste the heart
of your animal flower

i feel better when i'm busy i feel

better when i play my guitar
i feel better when i talk
to friends i feel better when i watch
the sky

i feel better when i take a walk i feel better
when i drink a glass of water

i feel better when i cook something good
when i don't think too much
i feel better when i stay in the moment
when i deal with what's in front
of me i feel better

when i'm busy
i feel better when i play my guitar
i'll feel better when all this
is over
please let it be over

i'll feel better
if this never ends

i remember when you remade me

in your image
made me feel as if i ruled
the universe
floated over the bloated planet
& everyone in it

      we made complicated decisions
      at the drop of a hat
      some days it rained hats

but now i'm small & fallen
all that petty history
a fragile fog
lost in wafer thin haze
& i wonder
who am i who are you & why
do we keep meeting
like this

o dear desire you overwhelm me
astound & overawe me
chew me up
& the rest of the scenery

      you underestimate your power
      to turn everything lost
      into paradise

thank you for pulling me

out of my emotional
                tailspin
& pushing me into another thank you
for showing me the difference
between material & spiritual
process & pain play
& performance
                art & death
thank you for not taking me
too seriously thank you
for the open heart surgery
thank you
for saving my life i was a wretch
when we met
broken thirsty needy hungry
now i'm nothing
yet i'm a satisfied nothing
thank you
for teaching me to revolve evolve
revert revisit rethink
reimagine
                let go
                let go
                let go
o dear desire
thank you for entering
& exiting on cue
i'll forever
carry you around
to remind
myself
how imperfectly perfect
we'll always be

the cage around my heart

now open
all the armor protecting
past removed
a new freedom slips
into bed
      warms me in the night
      alone
      with my endless thoughts
      & ancient memories
      the hum
            of the universe
            still searching for words
            to describe you
            dear desire
            how you conquered
            my every atom
                        launched me
      into orbit of beauty & ache
set the trap
then set me free

weight of the world

floating in
                    space

the gravity of the situation
no longer grave

inhale exhale

the only place in creation
now

letting go
          of the balloon

we rise together

a friend advised me

keep my hands off your stove
stay away from your range
out of your kitchen
run run run from your hearth

but dear desire i still feel your heat
still want to cook
on all your elements
sizzle on your surface & burn
myself where it hurts most

o that otherworldly fire
that dances us into each other

o pure passion flame
that tempts even temptation
scorches all logic
creates rings of blazing seduction
infernos that hypnotize & rise
higher & higher
drawing me closer
& closer

blinds me from danger
until i see only beauty
gives me visionless sight
that blinds me from beauty

step right up

stop throwing those baseballs
stop piercing those balloons
stop tossing those pennies
& rings

      i'm not a prize to be won
you said

i'm a lover not a loser i thought
and my heart wants
to win
wants to expand
even more
wants to give you
that larger than life panda bear
stay with you for a night
or a lifetime

      dear desire what does time
      matter

to a quantum lover

me

in the wide wide spectrum
of delusions
> you are my favorite
> nothing i can't accomplish
>> with you in my imagination
>> feeding me illusions
offering psychic encouragement
& me pretending
> you're always there
> that you really think of me
> & care
>> yet dear desire i know
>> i'm less than nothing
>> i've ceased to exist for you
i'm really out here
all alone
> so please excuse me for looking
> through reality
>> & wrapping myself
>> in the emotional blanket
> of our secret memories
> because
i believe it's not wrong
wanting someone to believe
> in the delusion of

me

spare change

life is about transition you said
& then you transitioned
away from me

once i was a god & everything
i touched turned to forgiveness

now i am broken in places
only the lost can find

all the goddesses i once kissed
have left my lips lonely

only you dear desire can begin
to know how much & how
little is gained

from wishing for want
& chasing your dream

a higher power

you make me jump with joy
you make me dance in space
& loop in time & loop
in time

i never stop loving
our loop in time

our space apart
our dance together
our jumps for joy
our loop de loop de loops
in time

dear desire may i remain
oblivious to oblivion
& never know
how much or how little
you believe in me

i'm in heaven thinking
the universe of you

as all my illusions dance
& loop & loop & dance
reaching & believing
in a higher power
of desire

know your limitations

for all your wiles & charms
your charisma & tricks
your female manipulations
your pretend poise & hot-button
passion

for each tender connection
a sharp word a hard
cut
a mad severing
of relationship strings

dear desire if only
i could remember how impossible
for you
to trust enough if
only i could

look into your eyes
& never forget
you cannot even wrap your
own heart
around yourself

you cannot make universal love
how confining
yet liberating to know you
can only create more
& more desire

yesterday a holy man told me

it's all suffering all of it
suffering
& it resonated so
i thought why can't i
suffer with you
                    dear desire
on a beach in hawaii
where surf breaks softly
breezes sing sweetly
& healing waves
roll in
forever
            teaching us the ride
is the answer
& the destination only
sand
only dust
only the distant echo
distant echo distant echo
of once mighty
mountains
                        i hear everything
                right now
        everything that makes sense
everything beautiful

& suffering

alas a loss aloof

they say when two hearts collide
magical portals open
& new worlds of possibility
are revealed

they say true love is forever
a high pure vibration
that goes on & on & on

they say when you dream
of someone they too
are dreaming of you

they say when consciousness
expands it cannot undo

o how they say so many things
dear desire do they also say them
to you? or do you somehow
stay above the fray?

how can you hover above
the physics of love?
just far enough beyond

the heavy gravity of longing
& eternal attraction

the wanting the wishing the waiting

beautiful illusions all exquisite
intricate interconnected
                traps we set
                to capture ourselves
with the wishing the waiting the wanting
in different sizes & colors
& shapes array
of styles & lust & sign
& cost
                each perfect in their delusions
                for the waiting the wanting
                the wishing goes on
& on & on
long after we let go
the molecules of memory
still hold power for you
& the wanting the waiting the wishing
                some want more some less
                but everyone wants
                the same thing
inside the wishing
the wanting the waiting
where everything vibrates
for you dear desire
                the moon the sun
                the stars all fall
in & out of orbit for each other
all dissolve & come
together
all return to you

give yourself permission to fail

she said not getting what you want
can be a very good thing he said
everything is temporary
but the moment she said if you want
to be a light you must first learn
how to burn he said turn on
your love-light she said turn it
all the way up
trying too hard is like teaching
the moon to dance he said
dance first dream later
is the natural order
she said wanting & not having
is the natural order he said
o dear desire so many things
are said but nothing is ever done
ever complete ever after

another form of suffering

we all have our skeletons & closets
& memory rugs
to sweep them under we all carry our crosses
& nooses & vices to support
our useless excuses

we all wear our battle scars & fears
& karma to prove we're all too human

except you dear desire you can change
everything with a smile
erase the slate of bad dreams
with your touch
wipe clean the chalk dust of lost
hope & lust with your lips

dissolve resolve absolve & never look back
your legs wrapped around my heart

or do i give you that power
to lay waste my own
my offering another form of suffering
my temple craving something
soft dark & bittersweet
something for my hungry tongue
to get lost in

prayer for desire

i will forever practice compassion toward you
fill up a billion bowls of holy thoughts
for you raise the sacred vessel
of my vibration
for you
breathe a hundred million prayers
for you to lift the veil of you sail away
from you stay far far away
from you have pity
& empathy for you
the no cure for you

o dear desire the depth of your shallowness
cannot open the cosmic gates for you
will never teach you
how to fly
never give you half
of what you take & one day the weight
of your great karmic wheel
will become
too heavy for you
to push uphill
will fold back on you & crush
all the dreams i once
dreamt too

meditation for desire

place mind in heart she said
& heal all wounds
erase the hurt
release all pain & bathe
in tranquility

breathe slow breathe deeply
breathe holy thru nose
& knowledge past throat
down deep down beyond words
beyond wind & fear & fact

beyond thought & wanting
beyond memory & dying
beyond sleep & time
beyond even you
dear desire

let our breath carry air & light
& endless life
deeper deepest down
filling lungs filling mind
expanding heart

radiating in & out
within & without breaking
any concept or cage
liberating control
releasing every limitation

shining the mind of the heart
opening the third eye
of every atom
dancing with universe
in every breath

o how i wanted

until want wanted more
& together we grew into an all-consuming
cosmos of want

but now dear desire
your power unplugged
your watch spring unwound
your byzantine combination picked
your controlling home undone
void of smoke
& funhouse mirrors

for in the end only love
conquers want & more

only love digests the reaching
the clutching holding on
& on & holding on too tight
till there's nothing
left to grasp

o love! the great gyroscope
of goddesses
high wire act of fearless faith
balancing & swallowing
mindless head with
open heart

prayer for openness

open mind open heart open field
open possibility open tranquility open
you open me

open thoughts open doors
open windows open house open
mouth open wide

open concept open relationship
open book open face open question

open note open swim open water
open ranks open wound open slowly
open early open often
open 24/7
open valley open vista open sky
open ears open eyes

open heart surgery open often
open mind open heart open field
open you open me

previous poetry collections
by Stephen Roxborough

luminosophy (2013)

this wonderful perpetual beautiful (2011)

son of blurst (2010)

blurst (2008)

impeach yourself! (2006)

so far all the very important
mind-expanding long ones (2002)

spiritual demons (2002) CD

making love in the war zone (2001)

Stephen Roxborough has been a backyard weedpuller, molybdenum mine mechanic's helper, two-time Canadian champion, tree surgeon assistant, librarian's aid, English major, art history minor, waterpolo goaltender, paper mill rollbucker, Eddie Silver & the Supersonics harp player, park attendant, photographer, skywatcher, adland copywriter, dishwasher, cross continent bicycle rider, marketing consultant, book reader, birdwatcher, bartender, art collector, stoveman, busboy, airline catering kitchen quality assurance, Las Vegas lifeguard, armchair philosopher, British champion, Buddhist monastery afternoon bellringer, movie house relief manager, right fielder, co-founder of a poetry festival, tree planter, house husband, food critic, frisbee tosser, book editor, photographer, bodysurfer, guitar noodler, ad agency creative director, vegetarian, dual citizen, Aladdin doorman, world traveler, meat cutter, artist, cook's helper, teacher, student, son, brother, father, lover, poet & hopeless romantic.

He was once fired for his too short haircut.

NeoPoiesis: *a new way of making*

1) in ancient Greece, poiesis referred to the process of making: creation - production - organization - formation - causation

2) a process that can be physical and spiritual, biological and intellectual, artistic and technological, material and teleological, efficient and formal

3) a means of modifying the environment and a method of organizing the self, the making of art and music and poetry, the fashioning of memory and history and philosophy, the construction of perception and expression and reality

4) an independent publisher with a steadfast goal to print and promote outstanding poets, writers and artists that reflect the creative drive and spirit of the new electronic landscape

NeoPoiesisPress.com

www.ingramcontent.com/pod-product-compliance
Lightning Source LLC
Chambersburg PA
CBHW031132090426
42738CB00008B/1061